Jesse –

To my close
friend ―
men...
my gu...
"Laugh a li...
when we are
together." I
absolutely
adore you,
Hise.

Love,
Marilyn

STILL WATER

Art Garfunkel

STILL WATER

Prose Poems

E. P. DUTTON   NEW YORK

Published in the United States by E. P. Dutton,
a division of Penguin Books USA Inc.,
2 Park Avenue, New York, N.Y. 10016.

Published simultaneously in Canada
by Fitzhenry and Whiteside, Limited, Toronto.

Library of Congress Cataloging-in-Publication Data

Garfunkel, Art.
Still water : prose poems / Art Garfunkel.—1st ed.
p. cm.
ISBN 0-525-24795-5
I. Title.
PS3557.A7154S75 1989
811'.54—dc 19 89-1091
CIP

10 9 8 7 6 5 4 3 2 1

First Edition

Portions of the lyrics from "Wish You Were Here" by Harold Rome,
appearing on page 34, © 1952 Chappell & Co. (renewed).
Used by permission. All rights reserved.

Hand-lettered poem numbers, hand-lettered part titles, and diagram
on last page are by Art Garfunkel.

Thank you, Jules, Gayle, Kim, for your support.

CONTENTS

I: EARTH

INTERVIEW
3

Poems 1–23
8

II: WATER

INTERVIEW
37

Poems 24–48
42

III: AIR

INTERVIEW
73

Poems 49–65
77

IV: FIRE

INTERVIEW
97

Poems 66–84
99

1: EARTH

INTERVIEWER: When did your interest in music begin?

ART GARFUNKEL: Music came to me because it was around the house. My parents sang; we had a wire recorder in the Forties; so I just sang because I had a voice, and realized it at age four, and because I had the example of harmony from my parents. I would sing to myself as I was walking to school, and I would sing as if I were preparing to be a singer. I remember singing a song and doing it again in a higher key, walking to school in first grade. I must have been working on getting my range higher. I would sing songs by the Crew Cuts, or the inspirational ones like "You'll Never Walk Alone." I guess I was waiting for rock 'n' roll to happen, which hit the radio when I was thirteen. I had just become friends with Paul Simon, my neighbor; we were in school together, so we both jumped on singing and listening to rock 'n' roll.

I: How old were you when you first performed?

AG: I first performed in talent shows when I was a fourth grader; I must have been nine. As I formed a friendship with Paul in junior high school we would sing in school, and we started doing the songs we wrote. Then we would go into the city and make demonstration records of our songs.

I: Did you ever envision that you would be well known?

AG: When I was around eight, the idea of being famous seemed like a big kick. And I knew I had a voice, and that it was a good voice. When I was in my early teens and heard records on the radio that Alan Freed was playing, I thought, I can do that; I can compete with that level of tightness . . . And I practiced constantly with Paul with a competitive instinct. By the teens I knew I had a shot at the charts. So, in my early years I must have wished to transcend the neighborhood; to justify my "weirdness" in the neighborhood.

I: You mentioned finding the perfect place for a good echo.
AG: This is a complex notion. Singers love the reverb, or the bounce-off-the-wall echo effect; it puts sustain on your notes. The modern era of the recording industry, since "Vaya con Dios," is largely about playing with echo and reverb. So I've worked with echo as if it has been my singing partner as early as I can remember; I'd sing in a stairwell, or any bathroom with tiles. Recently I was singing in Central Park under one of those viaducts, and as I centered myself along the axis of the tunnel I realized there was a remarkable echo if one was lined up right in the middle. Then I started to think that possibly the shape of the sounding chamber in the throat and mouth was repeated in the roof of the tunnel, so you were producing a sound from vocal cords to mouth chamber to tunnel chamber, and the shape was a repeat on a larger scale. I thought possibly that was the reason why the tunnel gave such a good echo.

I: You mentioned that in your trip to Japan, the best part of the day was being able to sing as loudly as you wanted, with no one around to hear. Is it a relief not to have to perform when you sing?

AG: I sing because it gives me pleasure to hear it when it's right. I always bring a kind of shyness to the experience when I sing in front of people, because I'm more comfortable as a singer producing a sound that my own ears enjoy. If others want to listen to it, they may, but I'm not altering my posture toward them. This is why a recording studio is ideal for me: you perform in front of a mike with no one around, against your own standards. That to me is a more comfortable thing than stage work. Privacy goes with singing.

I: You say that you bring shyness to your music. How difficult was it to decide to publish your poems, and was there anything that made you start thinking along that direction?

AG: At some point I was bitten by the inspiration to write. You keep doing it; it takes hold of you. There is no ulterior motive other than that an idea wants to get expressed. So the initial impulse has taken care of itself. But at a certain point, you say, "Who am I writing this to?" Since I had the initial inspiration and finished it, who was that for? Was it the therapy of getting something out that needed to be said? Or is it simply, I am seeing who I am, or what's going on in me, crystallized on paper? You realize you're writing to someone, even if it's to a soulmate you're hoping to find. Then you realize: Okay, I'm writing to others. But you think, Which others? How many others? So you think: Okay, I'll send them to friends of mine, so they can know a little better what I'm about. Then you think, I'll send them out in general.

In childhood, the music was born out of the fact that I can sing. With writing, I just had to write these things. With encouragement of various people, I have dared to put them out.

I: A fair amount of the poems deal with the loss, through suicide, of someone you loved very much. Did it help to write about her?

AG: She died in the late Seventies, and I began to write in '83. It became the thing I most wanted to talk about, the thing that was strongest in me. You have many thoughts about someone who leaves you. You know, I'm a great fan of J. S. Bach. Bach left us; but he left behind tremendous work. She left me her journals and memories and pictures, and in 1980 I was not so much hung up as I was a commemorator and an appreciator. I spent a lot of time with her greatness, after the fact; the same way I would if I were uncovering Bach's manuscripts after he departed. There was that aspect of the loss, because she was so fabulous to me. Then, there was the day I realized, I'll never get over this. Because "getting over it" is synonymous with sweeping the memory under the rug and getting on with life. I kept honoring her, thinking, I'm just giving credit where credit is due.

I: But then did you feel that life wasn't going forward for you?

AG: That's what they said to me then, and I would say, "Well, what do you think life is for, why is this a wrong way to spend my time? Should I be putting aside this acquaintanceship I'm immersed in, with her journals and books,

6

so I can get on to being acquainted with Dan Rather's six o'clock news? Is that what I should do? Get on with the culture I live in?"

Time can put you in a slightly different place, from which you'll have different feelings about the same things. Sometimes I think: We're born and we encounter living on earth. We encounter it from all the 360 degrees until we die. It stays the same; only the vantage point changes: a nine-year-old's; a twenty-nine-year-old's; a sixty-nine-year-old's—and loss is in it. The zebra is the same zebra; we just get to see it from all the angles.

1

Shot from guns, I disembark the world,
dropping digits from the urban population
count: from ten million London (8 figures) I
jet to Lyon (7), train to Chambéry, where I
stay the night in the 6-figure town. Then the
morning train to Bourg St. Maurice—5,
and taxi to Les Arcs, modern ski spa for
some thousands; in the Hotel Cachette—3, I
sign my name amid the lobby population
(more than ten) waiting to view the moun-
tains from my room . . .

It is midday, bright and brilliant.
Just the three of us.

Les Arcs, France   *December 1983*

8

2

Then I'll
Change my look to butterscotch,
    to russet, roan, and apricot;
And tie a chequered ascot shot
    with gold and auburn thread;

I'll wear a terra-cotta tan;
    and carrottopped and gingery—
A toasted almond man—I'll be
    in ocher in my head.

Not brown, but burnt sienna suede—
    my winter coat, the warm-up kind—
Not down, but plainly made and lined
    with ironrust instead;

And I'll not come too close to red,
    but stay the orange side and think
        that once I read Pink
            Beauty in her blushing cheek
    and now she's dead.

Les Arcs, France   *December 1983*

9

3

I am sorely waiting for my own applause to end in the headset, as I walk the Val d'Isère. There, I just discovered at the end of my performance at the London show last week—were three Christian hymns. I had missed these what with worry for the Webb piece, at the time. Indeed, I had missed my entire beloved Christmas in New York this year. (I like to sing the carols to myself as I pass the church at Fifth and Fifty-fifth.)

But I had laid provisions.

It is January 2, 1984. I am walking into Bourg. The pass to Italia below Mont Blanc is behind me. *The Animals' Christmas* finally fades.

Then Once in Royal David's City all those English Christian children little copperfields of praise—O Earth You are too wonderful for anyone to see—I walk among the traffic, The First Noël and swelled apart, the chambers of my heart, I am led beside the waters and I start to sing O Come All Ye Faithful We Live in Astonishing Splendor for Only a Moment Anointed in Oil and We Toil with Our Burning Glorious Bird-yearning Hearts!

Les Arcs, France   January 1984

10

4

O Kathryn, I kissed you goodbye.

You were wearing a white cotton dress with pale
    pink satin.
You were in the corner of the limousine, thirty
    minutes ago.

Outside the car, on the sidewalk, it was 4:40,
    Saturday afternoon.
Gorgeous, radiant sunshine fell on daddy and me.

It was the very middle of May.

How you delighted me all day long . . . You were
like a brook. And like a running mountain
brook you caught and reflected the
dazzling light.

You arrived cautious and curious. You had been
shopping for smells, and you bought a bubble-gum-
smelling eraser, a rootbeer lip gloss brush, a bottle
of cologne.

—Do you play chess? you said in the second minute.

At The Empire State, when we hit the big view at
the top—you took it in your own time. You were
Loch Lomond.

You like: typewriters, jigsaw puzzles, chocolate, pianos, grape soda, three in a phone booth, Pez, playgrounds and limousines. And most of all, it seemed, was playgrounds—the carriage ride we took to the carousel (where you rode the inside horse) charmed your daddy and me

but the playground was the cat's whiskers to you. I tried to sign your nose . . . Kathryn, thank you so much for giving me

Outside, daddy was saying "She'll never be five again."
So my goodbye kiss is to the beautiful wake you leave behind your beautiful course Kathryn.

the tribute of the current to the source

New York City   May 1981

5

2 Champs, late in the night,
    were up to their 18th tequila.
The wit, the rapport, the use of the metaphor
    made throwing up out of the question.

See them now:
    4 in the morning, the room reeling,
guitar playing,
    waves of nausea filling the songs.
Terrible, private pain.

There was a point of no return
    which he and I did pass;
The tickle of the tonsils—the old heave-ho?
    We both said No and kept the rage to ride that
coil of agony through the sunrise in the park . . .

They cheered for us in the baseball parks;
We strove for the hangover stage.

New York City   October 1983

6

Write the poem out loud.
Authorize the heart.
Burn the Bridge
and Be the work of art!

7

I will write my story backwards,
to February '79. To Laurie Bird,
when I saw her last in longjohns
red one-piece monkeybaby we said
goodbye one morning (was it March 3?)
in a fireplace room in Aspen. I flew off
to Vienna. I cross-country skied first at
the other end of Austria, practicing "Milena"
in the snow.

I spent four months with Milena—walked with her
to her chosen suicide attempt, in the story. Nic Roeg
led me.

But Phoenixlike she will rise in the final pages of my back-
wards book. Finally, what a sobbing writer I shall be then.
With resurrection music, with Phil Spector's "Old Man
River," I will reveal How great our love. How great my loss.

I'll span from here to there in sequence: cycle three of
Paul and Artie work (to stave off a stumble); excur-
sions in Europe; Alexandre Walker; fan mail;
my books; Central Park; *Scissors Cut;*
her diaries; my three-tiered "story"—
a)our four-year history, b)my life
Feb. to Aug. '79, c)the *Bad
Timing* script; her death;
our love; Her.

On a flight, LA to NYC   *January 1984*

15

8

The mountain road curves left.

I stop on the outside two-foot
    shoulder, looking down.

The motorcycle is heavy.

Getting ready to continue, I
    bend to my mirror to see if
    my helmetless hair is unruly—

But I must bend down to time
    and follow further down the
    crown my forehead makes at
    the top of the round rear mirror.

Alpine road   *September 1983*

16

9

There is a law to the descent.

First are the duck-pearl darts of purist light,
    a morning play in a glacial lake,
        trapped by the Alps at the top
           of the Albula Pass.

I make my resolve.

Then look up to see mountain scree
    and the beautiful alluvial fan.
        Scaleless.

Now begin the succulents. Antlered to
    the earth, following their spring
        fed courses—mountain gorse
           amid the stone-gray world,
                they introduce autumnal
                    colors, tart in their
                        translucence.

The water falls on tumbled rocks.
    Foam in light.
        Bedazzling.

The eye of the mind is the home of delight.
The face of the soul.
The humbling book.

Who can retell the pleasure of the look below?
  What media coverage—the darting
    communion, the retinal flow—
      newsworthy scan of the scale
        of the air-blue valley below?

The skin of rock is hid beneath the forest now.
  The road and I in midlife bisect the
    pine trees' tilted field. Like
      Apollo following Daphne
        trapped in trees
          I too pine for Her
            in the ventilating cool.

Beneath the verdant brow, with drying teartracks
  braided on my cheek, I break
    the invocation in the clear.
              Caroling
      Bruegheling
              Allawalt!

Merovingian images . . . holiest history,
These are the upper meadows—

Albula Pass, Switzerland   September 1983

18

10

I remember the mother duck heading with her brood for the twilight cove, in Holland. A streetcar came named "Amsterdam." I caught it to my hotelegram. Call home. "Are you sitting down?" he said.

London   February 1984

19

11

Back in the Twentieth Century
(before all this purple argon light),
When incandescence lit the dark
And carriages were in the park,
Randy Newman in his prime,
Stanley Kubrick still alive—
That brilliant time
When Culture thrived
And birds still flew free
    in the streets of New York

New York City   *March 1984*

20

12

I've been lettering my album notes. It makes me think of when I was nine. My father first taught me to drive a car by sitting me on his lap (he took the foot pedals), and letting me take the wheel. The natural inclination was to peer over the Chrysler medallion and watch the flying centerline thirty feet ahead. But my father, in his wisdom of experience, told me to keep my eyes up, and look farther down the road. There was the revelation: if you take the longer view, the near at hand is done for you.

These letters require exactitude. But though the "o" has to crest at the height of the "i" (or to the nearest 128th of an inch), I do it by watching the end of the line, with a hand still before me that is not even mine.

New York City   July 1984

21

13

Here on the other side of 1983, I begin to let the year roll backward. Erosion becomes crystallization. That which eroded (which thrust into existence) becomes sudden destruction. And a death played forward is rebirth in reverse.

But most to the point of '83, to synergy from entropy—To trace the perfect circle, you must walk a narrow line, you must check tangential forces and repress the spiral instinct for the center. Ever observing the Master's fixed radius, forsaking the chord for the bow, till you go nuts, and you spring to the rest of your life, thinking—wheels are for wagons and wings are for flight!

Now what does all this look like backward:

A free wide ranging peregrine will leave the sky to alight on the wheel of a Jaguar. The vantage point from the left rear wheel to the driver (an old friend of the hitchhiking bird) leaves a lot to be desired in case something need be said. Sure enough, there's misalignment in the vehicle. By the millionth revolution on the axle's eccentricity, the wheel itself is bent, the metal burning.

But heart like a wheel will go back to the cooling contemplation of the circle.

January, 1983: with tremulous cords, with my own latest highest evolvement of a life of devotion to beauty, with a comprehending glance into the deep of an unfilled well, I mounted the circumference of his disc.

New York City   *March 1984*

23

14

Say the soul is like fire: existence within us flickers and moves constantly uncapturable. Say the speed of successive impulses is six-per-second. Comes along a singer with a fine vibrato. The pulses are quick and subtle (sometimes mercerated, heaven-sent). They are the minute variations of pitch in the production of tone (we waverers, straddlers of Truth). Now, if their rapidity were, say, twenty-per-second, could they not remind us of the inner flickering Life force, stirred and directed toward our essence? It is the sharing.

New York City   *February 1984*

15

Between the winter solstice and the vernal equinox the
sun only rises to forty degrees, at this latitude in New York. At
two pm, I throw a ten-foot shadow on the promenade above
the East River Drive. Manhattan Island, tilted slightly clock-
wise on the map, is bathed on its axis in harsh winter light. So
that looking south down the river . . .

In architecture school, they taught us how to draw
perspectives: establish the horizon line and place on
it the vanishing point. (This is the point to which
all lines running parallel and exactly away from me
converge.) Thus Queens from the left, southbound traf-
fic on the right, Roosevelt Island, and in the gleam-
ing river—a southbound tug below me churns the sun-
lit foam as it ascends to vanish in the sea . . .

An old man in charcoal gray crosses in front of my
vision. Why is his parallel askewed to the pecture?
Is it the Doppler effect of visual nearness?

New York City   February 1984

25

16

Felix had a taste for marijuana.

Most every day he'd roll himself a joint.

One day in April, a young man with a social aware-
ness, with a Marxist interpretation of unfairness,
was driving a taxi through midtown Manhattan.
Felix was the fare.

The driver had been a philosophy major in his Cor-
nell days, then a social worker in New York. Now
driving Felix home through the park, he talked
about America:

—We were right in the Sixties. But the failure to
take the spirit and put it into a program, has led to
diffusion, distraction and cynicism for fourteen
years.

Felix thought of the tails side of the coin whose
heads is getting stoned—the generation's singular
contribution to middle class history—Is it not this at
the crux: to be high is to *video* life and to step back
from immersion within.

New York City   April 1984

26

17

I forget the thread New York makes through my life—a taxi down Park Avenue brings a flood of ancient memories:

Fifty-third and Winter of '62. I was at Columbia in those days. The Placement Office had this Christmas job in the Seagrams Building. Too poor not to make money at Christmastime, I applied for the job and got it . . . So there I was—in the basement, sorting packages— No, there we were, old Lionel Wick and me trying to get him to teach me Italian. We didn't care what we seemed like, to us we were working in Mies' space, contained by the travertine . . .

walk me down Park, pass *Carnal Knowledge* to

September, '69 and Fifty-first. I was recording "Bridge over Troubled Water" for CBS. Columbia back then. Over three hundred takes of my vocals are in the can, I can't get the first verse to properly set up the last which is done (which I like). On a break from the mike, I take my frustration to a church down the block, St. Bartholomew's Greek Orthodox—you've seen it there, set back a bit . . . So there I was in a pew facing east, seven years later and two blocks south, not exactly praying in the afternoon. I didn't care what I looked like, I was listening to You, containing the music.

I love this town. But nothing did I ever love as much as Her . . .
so who cares that the show must go on or that sadness fits for
the part?

We were shooting the final scene: an actor comes out
of the Waldorf-Astoria, 1979. He passes his star from
Vienna and sees the new scar on her neck. He gets
into a taxi . . . There I am leaving Park and Fiftieth,
joining the uptown flood. Beyond irony, the camera-
man's eye on a level with me, I am looking back at
the recent past, drawing the thread.

New York City   *March 1984*

28

18

A wishbone was broken.
I am holding the smaller part.
She, left with the larger clavicle
    (over the heart of the bird?)
    is having her wish.

New York City   *February 1984*

19

— See those two girls driving
    behind us—Alex, they're follow-
    ing you.
— No, it's you they're follow-
    ing; you're the driver.
— But you've got the long hair,
    that's what they like.
— But you have the famous face.
— But you've got the youth.
— But you have the money.
— But you have the beauty,
    and he let me end with the truth.

New York City   April 1984

20

Roy and I spent the last week in the control room at Regent, stringing together the best fourteen cuts from my five solo albums. When the assemblage was complete we got ready for The Big Playback. Pulling up my chair to the padded edge of the console, then centered between the speakers, I allowed myself to pretend I was a fan and turned the level up. I was one of two couples in a car headed for the country, early in the day. Someone popped in G's new cassette, saying "I like him" and "Bright Eyes" began. Then we all fell silent . . . and actually listened (enjoying the sight of the trees all the more). One of the girls says, in the middle of the first verse, "Turn it up." The fan in the passenger seat thinks, "What about this guy?"

London   *April 1984*

31

21

She took her tea weak with milk, often with
goat cheese spread on toast.

In the morning at the table, her beautiful
form beneath batik, she talked softly to me,
with a tiny crumb around her mouth.

Her lips were wet with tea

how unbearably kissable that region of her
breath

the center of my existence.

London   April 1984

22

We both had cotton T-shirts from Redfish Lake in Idaho, mine green, hers white. We had had them from before we met . . . At night in our bliss, she slept in only this, the captured sailfish nestled across her perfect chest.

In the morning at the dawn of consciousness, I would nuzzle under her armpit where the blonde hair was. There, in her smell, was my elemental resting place, straddler of dreams and the day, I see that cotton short sleeve cut her beautiful bicep at the top. Under it within that crumpled skinny harbor, safe again in love's conviction, I long to return.

London   April 1984

33

23

Sometimes I unconsciously fall into song, and for years I have wondered, "Why that song? Why then?" Now I believe that it sometimes works like this:

> Random unconscious mentation contains moments of summation—we name our state of being to ourselves, as a momentary synthesis, a philosophic still: "Am I blue?" Often this summation comes close to a song phrase (specifically, its lyric) such as to trip off the singing of the phrase: "They're not making the skies so blue this year . . ."

I pull up to TWA at JFK. It is July 4. I am going to Juneau. Awkwardly, I follow my suitcase from the car to the curb. I pick it up; I carry on. I sing the bridge of "Yesterday."

New York City   July 1984

II: WATER

INTERVIEWER: You're involved in an interesting project: walking all the way across the country. What route are you following?

ART GARFUNKEL: I left my apartment several years ago and first headed due west along the same latitude line, just to get a slice of America, traveling slowly on foot, to have more time to think, and to sing, and to write. As I continued, the changes of itinerary just came to me; I began to drift to the south. Lately I've thought, Am I headed for the Pacific in California, or British Columbia . . . ? It's somewhat arbitrary. It started when I went to Japan a few years ago. I took a freighter across the Pacific and went to Yokohama. I traveled alone, and when I got to Japan I decided to see the country on foot, since I'd never been there. I checked what little baggage I had into the hotel I'd arrived at, and I traveled as if I were new to earth. Except for the fact that I was upright instead of on all fours, it was a bit like crawling out of your playpen, wandering and wondering.

I: Did you know any Japanese before you went there?

AG: I studied on the freighter going over, so I had just a little facility in speaking it. And I could read the road signs.

I: Did you get into any trouble, being alone without much knowledge of the language?

AG: By the end of the first day I was about twenty miles out and I needed a place to stay, so I stopped at an inn and in a charade-like kind of English I asked for a room. She sent me away, so I hitched back to my original hotel. When I later looked up the word she had used when she called her husband up about me, it was *alone*. They must have thought that was too strange, someone traveling on foot alone. I set out the next day, and when I needed a room again I just relied on the human common denominator of a smile. I didn't have any problems after that. I was never desperate; there was always a place to stay. You can always shift for yourself; take a chance and it'll work.

I: Some of the Japanese people along the way recognized you. Was that an odd feeling?

AG: It's always amusing; it's fun, the celebrity trip I've been on for twenty-something years. It's a constant party of a kind. It's a potential magical encounter with everyone. A fan meets a hero, he knows him from the albums. They start off with "Are you who I think you are?" or "Can I have your autograph?" They're open to whatever the exchange may be. I often get very probing. I get into surprisingly serious conversations, things that in the normal course of socializing you'd back off from. But you find people say, "Well, it's a celebrity situation, I'll say things I wouldn't normally say." For years I've been using the vantage point of the celebrity life to be curious about people. You can be a reporter. They're getting a kick out of meeting you, but you're using the celebrity thing to really make contact with them.

As a kid I was a loner. When I achieved public recognition, it was a huge stroke of affection, and it gave me an "in" with which to make contact with people.

I: Does it often happen that the celebrityhood becomes intrusive?

AG: That's the other half of it. After the initial years, I started noticing that many situations come with terrible timing. It's interruptive. What's really tough is that it often interrupts the quality of the time you have with a friend. Say, a friend is now explaining to you what it was that's always been hurting him or her about something you have always done. And it's a quality understanding, you really don't want interruption. But as a celebrity, you're always a walking target. And you really are required to have your grace about it; they don't know what they're interrupting. You can lose some of your private life to it, but then again the phone does the same thing.

I: To get back to your trip across the country—will you eventually go west? You travel what, about two days at a time?

AG: I leave my house, I fly out to the state where I last left off on my walk, and I rent a car at the airport and drive to my last spot, then I do about a week of walking, covering 100 to 120 miles. In general, I'm doing the smallest paved road that takes me west.

I: So you really get to see backyards, you're really seeing America.

AG: In part, I'm seeing how uninspired America is. The landscape seems to change with time much more rapidly than I thought. I try to look at what is no longer on earth, things that existed up until just recently. Unless we try to notice the absence of things, they'll just slip away.

I: Do you see a lot of decomposing small towns, ways of life that are no longer extant?

AG: They've all gone to the cities. Small towns do not look charmingly small; they look sadly departed-from. Evidently the power of television or pop culture has pulled all the young people toward the cities.

I: Everything is so homogenized; regional accents hardly exist anymore.

AG: Why did we go this way? Is this homogenization the by-product of "Business comes first; the home office and its headquarters needed to call the country one single unit"?

I: Do people see you on their street and say, "Hey, there's Art Garfunkel"?

AG: They often assume, "It couldn't be him." I often play this game: I say, "What would he be doing here? Besides, isn't he taller?" They seem to agree. Then maybe I'll say, "Should I feel flattered? What's he like? Where does he live?" I want them to say: "I know who you are; what is it like to be a celebrity? What makes it different from my life?" That would be the most direct expression of natural curiosity.

I: What would you say to give them a sense of what it's like?

AG: Well, it's way more good than bad to achieve public recognition for singing. When people talk about the price of fame or the difficulties, they are certainly describing the minor aspects of it all. There are many positive things: the chance to express yourself, the ability to get closer to the back room. It increases awareness of how things work.

I: So other famous people who claim it's so horrible to be a celebrity . . .

AG: They *lie*. Nobody gets onto the top of the charts by accident. There's no one who was ever dragged there, or woke up there. They have rehearsed, and they have set out to match a vision of, as Norman Podhoretz said, "making it." You often see the celebrity hating the intrusion, or the incredible latitude the press has. But basically, being famous increases one's personal power enormously.

24

The ocean.
Why does it do this wonderful thing to me?
Would it not be the same if I sat on the end
    of my own woven carpet of boundless blue dimension—
        undulate, and empty of intrusion?
And if a silk ripple stole me
    and slid me stilly,
        slowly from hem to hem—then
Oceanworks!
Would I not feel them?

Atlantic Ocean   *July 1984*

25

There's more to Gayle and I than meets the eye.

She first appears in Maxfield Bleu where sweaters were three hundred dollars apiece; it was 1978. With her heart breaking—her Great Love gone away— what was she doing there, new to LA? Was it ingra- tiation? Was it Tommy, the clothing salesman? Was it Carly in the shop trying dresses just then
                        when the Bird dropped in.

Life being Love to her, Laurie felt pushed away by the G.
—No air supply he, thought she of his need to finish his album alone, and she quickly prepared to fend for herself . . . telling Carly what looked good on her and lots of what did not . . . Tommy pretended to own the store and basically kicked the Bird out the door. But

Gayle's heart was offended. She defended frailty. That's how Laurie befriended Gayle.

Now that it's six years later, I think of the time of *Watermark*—the start of the mix when *I* chose to go it alone—
Was Laurie a lure?
Was she the flighted Mercury that brings news of Venus waiting in the wings? Could all her beauty be Love's page at dawn—a morning rooster Kyrie to the Glory in the rest of Love's full day?

North Atlantic   *July 1984*

26

I walk the ship from end to end,
    watching it part the waves.
A part of loving is knowing . . .
    water excited. diaphanous folds
I have come to know somewhat the sight
    of the beautiful foam below.
Now the courtship continues
    to sail amid marble.
I look for my love to grow.

Atlantic crossing   *July 1984*

27

Was it not Thursday I writhed in pain while
the Walkman played for distraction? Dante's
Inferno was on . . . "Midway along the path-
way of our lives" . . . Blood stained the bed,
but Virgil-led I succumb to the land of the
lunatic cries of the doomed in a death that
never dies.

Out of the throbbing pain in my bed,
    I refine the anomaly—
Fired in irony, dreamed in dread,
    I divine comedy.

Atlantic crossing   *July 1984*

28

We make a "V" the moon and me
      and the moonlight on the sea.
The angle of incidence carries the eye
      down a moonbeam valley
      and then to the sky.
When she first appears,
      our two careers are gently inclined
      to horizon love;
But when she's high
      and her glow nearby,
      we're a steeple inverted
      with a moonstone above.

Atlantic crossing   *July 1984*

29

I go to sea because I take too much for granted. Beyond education there really is this spinning sphere in space. And we're all on it spinning and sliding in relativity. You and me.

Forget the endlessness. At best we're just a Spalding in a mausoleum; we're the powder on the ball.

We're a chip of stonework slowly falling from a vaulting rib, The Milky Way, in a chancel bay of the Notre Dame. In clerestory light, on the deck in the night I see that Gothic Rib—like chalkdust it stripes the entire dome, a trick or treat of countless spheres at the end of the eye's discernment. Me and the firmament all in a galaxy, tinsel chips on a pinwheel blade.

Atlantic crossing   July 1984

It is an overcast night, but Bob and I are huddled in the wheelhouse, thirteen feet from the wheel. Only the desklight on this great center table that fills up a third of this spacious room is on. Lit by it, sits the Atlantic chart and a pencil line of our course made good.

Bob and I are in celestial wonder. The heavens revolve from east to west. We follow the Dipper, it leads to Polaris, and then he says this to me next:

—Now the North Star is the only star that stays fixed in the sky through the night. And its altitude in the sky is your latitude on earth.

I am stirred to the core. He has given me the night's compass, a nocturnal bearing on everything. This polestar and I will make an axis in space, we'll split the face of the sky in two. Forevermore, when I see it above the horizon—a portion of ninety from level to plumb (my selfsame proportion from equator to pole)—then the whole poem-dumb world, the dome of pearl zodiac, Polaris and me and seed to stem, the rolling Sistine starscape will enwrap them.

Under blankets as a child, I would stare at the ceiling molding over me. The eye would slide, then the molding took a hold of me. Under a porthole now, in bed, the universe is more a home to me.

North Atlantic crossing   July 1984

31

I catch myself in close-up looking into three con-
centric rings.

If they combed the world to find me, covered all my
stomping grounds on land and raked the sea—
(only at longitude seventeen west
   and latitude forty-eight north,
four hundred miles from the Brittany coast
   in the hull of a night-riding voyager,
loitering in the pantry
   spooning pear juice from a tin,
remembering her love for pears,
   and staring at rings in a tin sea,
      would they find me)

Atlantic Ocean   *July 1984*

32

Jeff takes me down to the bottom of the ship.
There, amid the massive turbine, the reduction
    gears, the great propeller shaft—
Thirty-five thousand horses are pulling a
    guided tour.
The young apprentice stands on the keel and
    I am here to learn;
I feel his need of our script to succeed.
I see in the eyes the fear of concern.
He has taken the reins of the foreman's role
    with his first fragile grip;
I cast for clues—a tip—
    the slightly trembling upper lip,
    the fish beneath the ship
    a foot below our shoes.

Atlantic crossing   *July 1984*

33

Some like to use a picture frame to hold the composition.
Others are less structured, and deal in intuition. But I am like
Nicolas Roeg: "There are no endings," just this bolt of cloth;
we stitch designs and then we cut them off and we leave raveled
threads dangling . . .

I hang above the barge bay in the last day's sunset.
Suds in a hairnet of aquamarine in an onyx ravine
between England and France are dancing in the unraveling.
I cut a section through my life at zero longitude along
the weft, and retrospect on loose threads . . .

They are heartstrings, most of them. Elective affinities.
Things we tend to lovingly from day to day:
the new black sleeveless vest my mother made;
the Captain's face of amusing grace and sly;
these old containers—loaves of the merchant trade;
my new relationship with the night sky;
that piece of ocean—a dash at a hundred degrees;
the cells of the skin of cadets in the folds of the eye;
these words, this book undertook to please
Celestial Cassiopeia,

                                    I kiss the hem of your nightgown.
Commanded by you: "Some things you may not forget." It
was the fabric from *your* loom that put me here on this ship at
the stern these years in the white water wake;
It is for your sake that I try to make a peace with the
cutting shears
and go on spinning the filament for you;
a stevedore adoring in the breeze

on the flying bridge—the surge—the slit—
the fibrous flood—the leap of blood from what
the heart can't help but love . . . cords dangling
the private pounding passion of regret

Leaving you to weave the rest, I offer these

Atlantic Ocean   *July 1984*

34

I walk to Foyle's, the bookshop. When I get to Charing Cross Road, green leaves are on the few remaining trees standing there . . . at Denmark Street.

Twenty-one summers ago I came to know this part of town. We sang Paul Simon songs and passed the hat around at Leicester Square. Kathy collected. She was seventeen. We were twenty-two then, and for a lovely little while.

We were new to the plural of holiday; you went on them on the continent as a rule. In those days you knew a thousand things to do to be cool . . . It's not so much that leaves turn brown, it's the trees themselves that are taken down, leaving a void around Foyle's for me to understand. Once, my heart was filled with the love of a girl and the whole lush grove of the world was expanding

Today, green leaves are on the few remaining trees of Denmark Street still standing.

London   August 1984

35

Good Friday. I took a taxi to Chelmsford, then walked to the North Sea. It is spring. I had my homework in the Walkman.

I walked along a path beside a canal, singing and thinking of her again:

If she were a "tabula rasa" and I a believer in all in the eye of beholding, then what she was was what I saw; her power, my capacity.

She was a mirror and I saw myself more kindly. And she took me up.

Chelmsford, England   April 1984

36

Cockfighter, the movie; "Rooster Village," her jacket; there's been a rooster reverie running with me.

Perhaps it started with Joyce last year and his "husbandly hand under hen." Then the rooster appeared as a bird to me, an odd one, but all the same a bird . . . a word more than game to me, the bantam quality provoking me, the red comb dangling, tickling me with the thought of genitalia, the rude erection of the rooster's neck—the tearing cry of her morning call—all fierce expressions of the spirit of the bird, *la gloire,* the French would say.

Today I passed the chantecler at the Ambassade d'Angleterre atop the gate in gold. Angry like the eagle, released from barnyard play, the rude bird rips the daybreak calm with torch-fire, mixing memory, brave and pathetic, with desire.

Paris   August 1984

37

Show me an Andrew I'll show you a prince of a lad. We inhabit our names and the images of our names: the image of Priscilla, of Harry, of Wayne, the island of Skye, shelter from the storm but adjacent, rancor's raging scorn nearby. The picture of a boy under overcoats on a screened-in porch in a thunderstorm. He brings his chair to the edge of where rain invades, closer to the lightning and the spray. He is a stowaway, grown to manhood on bitterroot and goldenrod. Born to November ways, he travels north to Stornoway.

Fort William, Scotland   *August 1984*

38

Perhaps it's personality I've lost. Maybe in "works and plays well with others" I never earned my "s" (show me an Arthur who did). Not unlike Rimbaud I tend to go my own invented way, beyond fame. I live in soliloquy and I don't mind the wolf in me, nor all this rugged barren beauty 'round my shoulders, as I ride alone.

It is the eve of September, August thirty-first, that clearest cusp of the calendar. Autumn has begun in the Hebrides. The day has come to the end.

Nineteen hundred eighty-four kilometers of two-lane blacktop have passed from the rue du Faubourg St. Honoré, through the Bois de Boulogne, la porte de St. Cloud, Argenteuil, up the Seine, Veteuil, Rouen 'n onward west across Normandie, always in sunshine—Repentigny—kick into fifth to the ferry at St. Malo—then the Anglo-Saxon section commences: Southampton to Soho Square. (I interrupt to go to London on a train, to the art department at CBS, to Intourist . . .) Back to the bike and the south and the centerline, past Stonehenge, through the Cotswolds to Leeds, we weave around the spine of England's midlands to Northumberland in summer wind, and over the border to Scotland . . . there's no one in this country, pathetic little road, purple mountains heather and brown follow me down to the motorway to Glasgow—town of Scrooge and Marley buildings—built around the Eighties, empty since the Sixties, downtown Stonehenge, train station space that great place, I sit in the sunlit morning among men who don't work, with the Firth beside, birds gossip in the gleaming of the Clyde . . . and I am reading Edmund Wilson, listing north-northwest and dreaming beyond Lochs Lomond and Ness, over glenned loveliness to the serious beauty of the highlands. The clouds and I are attracted and held in thrall. It rains. Fall weather emerges at Invergarry and in reply we ride to the Atlantic on a ferry from the mainland to the Isle of Skye; keen is the air and keen the eye of the Scots; I write lots of postcards in a Portree laundromat and clean in the rain and then today, when with herring gulls we ferry to the Hebrides, sixteen minutes of one degree increase in latitude—platitudes, and how she doesn't talk to me—land in the minority, Uig to Tarbert, tarn island across the Little Minch. As Skye fades into water, its final fields in silhouette climb north-northwest to cliffy falls.

And I have come to Stornoway, 1984 away from Paris. Across the Isle of Lewis, and from its leeward side, I ride alone to the sea at last. Under a shelf of risen rain the northwest sun emerges and slips slowly on its way to set. Chastened and enchanted and forgiven again, a silhouette is slowly rising into it.

Stornoway, Scotland   *August 1984*

39

September 1. Stornoway.
The hotel manager asks me to sign
his cassette for him—*Scissors
Cut,* here at the end of Europe.
"God bless the romantics," he says,
while I sign my name.

Stornoway, Scotland   *September 1984*

Now imagine a scale with sunrise equal to birth.
Let a spring day begin at 7 am, and end in the
      night at 9; let 9 be set equal to death.
Imagine the life of a person was 84 years, and
      you have a proportional scale: 14 hours equal
      84 years.

I am a middle child, 42.
In a muddle in the middle of the middle, it is
      2 in the afternoon for me.
At twenty-to-two I am walking from the center of
      Sheffield to the hills in the west.
I'll only be out about 36 years, and return when
      the sun starts to fade.

I had breakfast in Queens;
      Spent the morning in school;
Fame struck at 11.
      Bridge played at noon.
Then I started the afternoon off with a marriage
      that lasted for twenty minutes.

Ten seconds before a quarter-to-one I fell deep-
      ly completely in love.
For forty minutes we lived by the sea and strayed
      among billowy clouds . . . being the day was young.

Now it's a quarter-to-three.
    I am under a tree in a town park.
The sun is still high, the day is sweet, and no-
    body thinks of the night now.
The years pass invisibly . . . a minute is 25 days.
What is to be done with the rest of the day?

Sheffield, England   April 1984

41

"You met me once before we met the first
time. It was at Cinema I or II in New York. I
was on line for *Swept Away* and you looked
me straight in the eyes then went away . . .
So years later, by the Bridge of Sighs, when
I saw you apart, I knew it was safe enough to
trust the consistent heart."

Milan, Italy   March 1986

42

These Russians want to know how rich I am.
    I study clothesline wardrobe as it dries.
We have a vital interest in each other
    and spheres of influence are in our eyes.

Nothing, from *The New York Times* to *Pravda,*
    of the starving for connection, do we learn.
I ask them who's their favorite U.S. actor.
    "Ronnie" is the answer they return.

Smolensk, USSR   *October 1984*

43

I walk down Nevsky Prospect. One attractive face—she flirts as we pass. It means a lot to me. Sun comes out over the Neva. Birds still fly free. On t.v. last night, Gromyko is shown with Reagan in the White House. G. looks mentally lively; R. is bitter-looking, phony-folksy. The editor's power.

At dinner, an electric guitar, a Fender Rhodes, bass, drum, and violin play "Moonglow," "I Left My Heart in San Francisco." The maître d' wants to know if I still sing with Mr. Simon or alone.

On Monday the authorities have decided to confiscate my undeclared money. Then they ask for an autograph.

I get stopped for jaywalking into the road to see if a taxi is free. Three rubles.

On the sixteen-hour train trip, my compartment mate is a military man. He changes from uniform to blue jogging suit. His book does not move one cm. over the centerline of the table between us.

It's all about my grandmother here. I see how very Russian she was. Tea in a metal holder, stern facial expression, a chicken's neck in the cabbage soup, *kasha,* the dryness of the liver, sturdy body frame, chess on t.v., the specific human sweat smell of the sleeping car.

Cigarette holders, lamé coats, San Remo Music Festival on t.v. (Russian voice-over), Gert Fröbe, the Refusenik in Minsk . . .

Leningrad, USSR   September 1984

44

DURATIONS:

1. inhale—exhale:	4 seconds
2. breakers on a shore:	10 seconds
3. wash and dry:	80 minutes
4. tide—neap and ebb:	6 hours
5. productive recording session:	12 hours
6. a cut healing:	8 days
7. leaves on a tree:	6 months
8. getting over a friend's abuse:	1–5 years
9. trouser cuffs—pegged to flared and back:	28 years
10. a civilization:	400 years
11. overcoming the loss of a true love:	eternity

Minsk, USSR   *October 1984*

45

Maybe life is like Lorne's bulletin board when he'd sit up there at Thirty Rock—Then put up the three-sixty-five, arrange them in their tribes, honor their traits and dwell in them cyclically, filling in dates, until life is full.

Put down June nineteen. (All, in time, are marking points, memories, memorials.) Call to mind the midnight moment—the first of the year. Think noon goes by where June meets July. And every clockwork month—two hours of the calendary day.

See me along a sliver of river, through Luxembourg city at five-to-one. The day is July eleven. I walk awaiting the first of spring, still encompassed by her ways: born in the week of the first of fall, suicide at summer's eve.

For nine point nine five years now, you have tyrannized my soul, usurped commemoration, stopped time still . . . and on my wrist you left the tick of history to beat . . . nineteen minutes to two o'clock . . . twenty days until we meet

Luxembourg   July 1985

46

Konstantin Chernenko is dead. I am the newsman. In my bedroom, I push off *An Actor Prepares* from the top of the television set and put up the tape deck, preparing to sing for my album.

Next week, the Wimbledon Kings College choir— two dozen fortune-bred boys of eleven singing the animals' witness to Christ in his birth. The week after, U Street in the ghetto of Washington, D.C. I play S. D. Blass, a somewhat has-been writer of the local daily news.

And I have Lisa for my muse now. And a vision of yesterday's sail. With a lantern up in the crucifix— its light and the wind shining into canvas, a 2-piece moonlit billowing, the papal hat of Corbu. On a course of two hundred sixty degrees from Raiatéa to Maupiti, in the Polynesian chain.

The stereo is perfect from the wheel in the stern. The wind is in my hands. Gregorian chants are in my ears. The setting moon lies north, northwest. Across the South Pacific laps a moonbeam to hold our direction by . . . and I am learning with my tutor on this enchanted evening turned to night. She teaches me to master the play of the flag in the masthead as she touches me below.

New York City   March 1985

47

Work in D.C. is through.
Back home in Central Park,
I accidentally intersect
The alternating current
Of a stranger's point of view
And the young man viewed.

He lies, wooed, in the grass,
His ass to the sun,
With only a bathing suit on.
He lets the rude intrusion of
The stranger's line of sight
Pass between his
Slightly parted knees.
Then, to tease the peeker,
He lifts his ass a millimeter,
Pleased to play the street cat
And be peeked at.

I see the charge go through his spine,
His eyes glued to beyond where mine can see.
What is he watching, this tom alert—
The art of atoms—a hope, a screen?
A conduit in the line of lewd electrons,
The love of seeing and of being seen.

I, the interloper, daring not
To intervene or be deterrent,
Or even attract the vector's splendor,
Prudently cross the current.

48

I seem to lean on old familiar ways.
Penny and I go to see Lorne and Susan.
Their neighbor drops by—
       the awaited accident.

Awkwardly, I make an early exit.
He follows me out of the living room.
I follow the heart again.
We talk; he listens.
Copernicus.
Kepler.
Sparkling foam washes an eroded shoreline.

New York City   May 1984

III: AIR

INTERVIEWER: How would you compare the creative processes of the things you've done: acting, writing music, writing a book?

ART GARFUNKEL: Well, I'm not a songwriter; I was when I was a teen-ager, but all the Simon and Garfunkel years, and all the years I've been making solo albums, I performed songs written by others. So therefore this book is really the first creation I've done in the sense of bringing a piece into existence from nothing. When I made the few movies I made, it was a thrill to be a researcher, a homework artist. Preparing what the character was about was great fun. In the process of shooting you are preparing your next day's lines; for me it was very similar to analysis. You're dealing with memories, and states of being, ways you've felt, things that have touched you, all related to what's in the shoot tomorrow. What's fascinating is that you uncover about nine different approaches to these same two pages of language; there are familiar and less familiar ways these things can be said. Writing is often a first line and a sense of where it's going; something you've thought about all your life that has finally crystallized for you.

I: In one of the poems, a cab driver says, "We were right in the Sixties." How do you think the spirit of the Sixties has evolved, and do you think there's any of it left?

AG: I've had to learn, to my great disenchantment, that what I felt as a twenty-year-old in the Sixties was an inspired energy boost, whereas I thought it was a cultural fact that would lead to a permanent shift in American life. I've had to deal with the disappointment that goes with seeing that that boost was simply a traditional young person's burst of optimism. While we were so convinced that our more open attitude toward finding meaning in life in the Sixties—while we were so fired up with that—even as we were, there were forty-five-year-olds who knew that it was something else, who perhaps had also been through a young period of spirit and had cashed in that point of view for financial security for the family. So they had experienced a personal shift, and we hadn't, because we were younger. So now I'm dealing with seeing that shift and wondering if this is a necessary aging phenomenon, or is it merely dropping the ball? Were we once, in the Sixties, young Americans at that time, were we not really on to something?

I: Do you think young people have dropped the ball nowadays?
AG: Well, we only see life from our own perspective. As I've gotten older, it does seem that the Seventies were a kind of nowhere, as if any inspiration of the Sixties did not lead anywhere. So I don't know if I'm typical of other Americans, but it seems we've been adrift and we lack inspiration. We're a nation that does not know what its direction and vision is, where it thinks it's going. We've had almost two decades of this now.

That's what I was talking about when I was saying that the Sixties seemed so alive with hope and change for America. But it's all from where you look at it. Do the seasons give me the same fulfillment as they did when I was young? I feel they're better than ever. What some

74

things mean to me seems to have been enriched through the years. If I take delight in the clarity of the air, that delight seems to be a richer thing than when I was younger. My very self is more than it was, so the apparatus with which I take in and put together and make meaning of anything seems worth more now.

I: You just got married, and you mentioned that you might want children. Do you have ideas about how you might want your children to be—in the light of disappointing recent generations, perhaps? Would you like to have a child who is musical?

AG: Interesting question. My natural inclination is to dare not put expectations on another live being. Because this word *freedom* is crucial. I live with a fair amount of personal freedom, and I find it's the air that I breathe to know that I can choose to find happiness in my own way and not worry about judgments or the image of my deeds. So before I get notions of what I hope for in another, I would rather check that. I hope for health in a child, but I really hope that they feel unencumbered by Daddy or Mommy's expectations. Sometimes when a parent is very hands-off, a child has an extra sense of wanting to satisfy him or her; it works in reverse. Because if the parent is so liberal, the child is so much swimming in free choice the child sleuths out what he thinks Mom and Dad would like him to do. If my child is musical or not musical, I think that's six of one, half a dozen of another. It's a very wide world. You want the kid's spirit to come out rather than be repressed. I think tolerance is a fabulous word. These are the only parameters. I don't want to be such a permissive parent that the kid doesn't feel there's some structure. So I think rearing children might—I've never done it, but I sense it's a lot about mixing freedom with structure. It's an art form, probably. And you just love the shit out of them.

I: Do you usually travel alone? I know you went to Alaska with your brothers.

AG: Half the time I'm alone, half the time not. I believe when you travel alone, you encounter the world more directly. But I do both. I go with Kim, I travel on motorcycles often. I love to get on a freighter, and I'll do that alone. A freighter trip is great for writing; it's just terrific. When you're on a freighter you really do not have to live on a twenty-four-hour schedule. You can hit a writing jag and do thirty-six hours of pacing the deck and being out under the stars and then go back to your room for more typing. And when that arc has been run, you can sleep for however long it takes.

49

Life is the spaces between. Anything fixed is false. Appearances approximate the things from which they emanate; so I hesitate to write to you.

Name it and it's somewhere else. How can you spell a tree? What can you say about you and me—that we stood on shaky ground when last we met? And yet—I firmly expect to share the embrace of reaffirming laughter in your face tomorrow and forever after.

London   July 1985

50

two tears,
        my own,
fell on my collarbone,
        roaming in shade in the north of France,
beneath where her shoulders meet—
Leonardoland, a hand in Lorraine,
        a foot in the Pyrenees.

But today is the first of June, Sunday,
        nearly twelve o'clock.
I am biking back to Paris from Bordeaux.
Woe is still with me
        here below Châteauroux.
Ancient Gallbladder rules.

Why should the plot destroy the panorama?
Isn't blood free to return to the heart?
Bilious or splenetic or in sanguinary humor,
        each in his craft or sullen art?

Then call me the breeze in the picture,
        and paint me in the center lane;
A triptych paneled in fields of grain,
        and hymns blown through me once again.

Romorantin, France   June 1985

78

51

Schoolgirls swinging,
    two on a swing,
Two-way momentum,
    thighs on thighs . . .
Each girl gets to
    look up at her mate,
They alternate
    against blue skies.

Ozark Mts., Arkansas   May 1986

52

A bird brooch broke some years ago:

I was about to tell Theresa, my co-star,
my dream of the night before
of the bird with the broken beak;
she was showing me the pin she wore—
a setup for a scene
in the fresh March morning,
there in Vienna was the bird
of my dream on her lapel.
When suddenly it fell.
The last one-fourth of the bird's
black beak had chipped away.
(Bury the point of her beautiful lips.
Pinocchio's lie is foretold.)

Into our mobile sound truck now comes
the untwisting—a visitation of the
vicar of St. Paul's.
The sixth spring since Vienna has begun.
So we play John Shepherd "The Carol of the Birds."
Inside his church, ten feet away,
two dozen lads have just finished
doubling their part:
        "One white, white bird . . ."
and at the very end:
        ". . . white bi - i - ird, white bi - i -"

The second engineer has cut the final word;
the last quarter of "bird" is erased.
(How beautiful it once had been, I muse in wonder)
Suddenly thunder.
Reverberant, I turn from the console
to the vicar across the camper—
I shall not want.

London   March 1985

53

When the day comes when, as a last resort, I take to the sea, wait for the sunset, smoke a first "j," walk the ship, and not have a thing to say . . . not be aware of tone, nor hear my own unique voice, pleased to be and to take inventory—then it's all over for me.

Atlantic crossing   July 1984

54

—I don't need to be reviewed out in the Pacific.
This, to me, is rude, I tell her; Who cares if he thinks
I'm unsociable—I didn't ask him to tell it to me!

The airy sea surrounds the two of us in cabin C.
She puts down her work,

—They ask about you, you know; they aksk
me if you talk to me when I'm fixin' up your room.
(How can I tell her how little I care, that her lips are
where my speech has landed, and so I say,)

—It's a funny way you have of mixing up the
"s" and "k" of "ask" as if an extra "k" were in it.

She smiles at my unasked-for observation and
drops the "aks" in "ask" again by accident while
quietly reminding me she didn't.

Pacific crossing   *July 1985*

55

It's not just for the rising time
    that shades are drawn
        to keep the light away;
It's for going to sleep near the end
    of a still-light day.

There, through the porthole,
    the darkening sky and I are companions
        in fading to black at sea;
Our rise and set—a synchronicity,

A new one on me: the shadeless night,
    so late in life to get to know
        and fall asleep in indigo.

Pacific crossing   *July 1985*

56

Two Japanese teenage boys—one, the attraction, the other, attracted, walked in sundown's afterglow around Tokyo. Having no better place to go, I turned around and followed them.

Maybe I am the attracted one—a stand-in beside the thin frame of the favored youth, as it glided within Hawaiian cotton that slid against his skin. No, his beauty must be featured in the feelings of his friend.

At the end of the street, a red light brings me closer to them. We wait (Where are we going?). I look into the crook behind the underarm of the chosen one, the taller of the pair, when the shorter brings his shoulder there—the finest point of contact, hardly aware, a hush . . . the unbearable lightness of being there, witness to the blush, the leaning in, Zen-gentle letting him.

The boy whose wardrobe is trying too hard adores his mate, and I can't help but empathize. Running down the ribcage and the tenderness of the inner arm, I feel the straddling security in the lengthening stoplight swoon . . . the permanent stain of affection as something *I* recognize.

Tokyo   August 1985

57

I remember this on-the-floor-living—woven mats, bright tan. Seven years ago, when I walked Japan, I came to an inn like this with a proprietress, comely and young. She fed me, and then she did my laundry.

In the morning she brought the clothes to my room. I stood on the tan and put on my cut-off jeans, while she on her knees observed to see if they'd shrunk. Loose threads hung down around the legs an inch or two.

Maybe she felt responsible for the stringiness caused by her wash; maybe her sense of service was refined; maybe it was lust that caused her to cut the cords with her teeth, from behind to my inner thigh . . . whatever it was, I didn't mind.

Hokkaido, Japan · *August 1985*

58

I plucked a dandelion, closed
my eyes and sniffed—there
were the St. Louis Cardinals
and the real Stan Musial up at
bat in Ebbet's Field shade,
hose of red and blue, ankle-
hoofed.

Shiretoko, Japan   August 1985

59

Overdubbing.
Into the heart of Nashville this morning I
brought Tolstoy—*Confession* (1879). Under
speckled autumn light, before the capitol
steps, I retraced with Leo his search for
faith—how urbanity, rationality, and the life
of wealth were obstacles in the pursuit.

Yesterday, Amy Grant sang on our album.
From out of church music she arrives at the
date addressing the singer's challenge at the
microphone—to offer the inner self.

And where is my faith? Has there not been
for me a loss in the meaning of everything
since the day she died?

Tolstoy toiled with the common man, an
attempt to be God's instrument. Amy came
with a student's air. And I employ these peo-
ple to come and put their feeling in the tape.

It has become a gothic cathedral to me,
this *Animals' Christmas*—an anachronism.
Jimmy and I are stonecutters, building a
structure in praise of God.

Nashville   October 1985

Three days of singing in Montserrat have passed.
Eighty percent of my work has been done. Under a
butternut tree, Ralph Vaughan Williams is playing. I
am a plumb bar swaying, yielding to the inclination
of the wind. Free to rotate, out on a limb, in a
hammock shaped like a sideways "J" and hung from
a single cord, I lean toward autobiography . . .
When the wind decides, it blows through the theme
by Thomas Tallis at the base of the tree and changes
the stereo on me.

Montserrat, British West Indies   *August 1985*

61

Sitting, working beside Geoff Emerick,
hearing him speak of the *"Pepper"* album, I
remember the age of excitement. The badge
is still in my fingernail . . . We were out to
dinner with Ringo and others—Laurie and
I, in Hollywood, Moroccan place, Dar Mar-
greb, with towels on our laps and pitchers of
margheritas. Very drunk, I go to hit the
head, and slam the bathroom door on my
nail.

Montserrat, British West Indies   *August 1985*

62

Now the side walls are going up.
Piano, harp and vibraphone in repeating
arpeggios are as masonry—a field of articulated lines.
Apertures left for a trumpet decree, a
cor anglais—
Strings and woodwinds finish the stone.
Through the clerestory, children's voices
descend upon David's City.
Around the base—a donkey motif like a
tom-tom frieze in low relief.
Stained glass windows, angel-drawn,
arrive at the site;
Echo and I are the colored light.

Montserrat, British West Indies   *October 1985*

Past striving, I continue to kick around. I've had career. I've been in love. Why persist?

Another "digital delinquency" has stopped the mix for almost a week. Buttresses, stepped and stone-finished, lie on the ground about to fly. I hang with the masons while I think about my life, my father, Children!
To complete my life?
To give the trip as a gift?
To not be the end to the branch of the tree
of genes?
What does it mean?

I fought with my father just last week and could have pulled the whole house down, ripped the charade of family apart, tired of being misunderstood. But I called him later and patched it up. Just why did I call?
For one of the ten commandments?
To teach my child to rise above?
For: Do unto others as you *will* have others
do unto you?
Or was it the genes we share?

Could it be that the way we wonder is
more alike than anyone else we know?

Montserrat, British West Indies   *October 1985*

92

64

A firefly flew
    into The Old Spanish Carol
To the amber light above and back.
It lit on the fader
    of the fourteenth track
        for a sit;

Where Ossian Davis
    had played his harp
On Christmas Eve a year ago;
Where Geoff just mixed
    the instrument low
(or lower perhaps than the
    firefly felt it should go)

What is it trying to tell us—
That it knows where the focal points are?
That its insect heart is set
    on the part of the star?

Is it just a nightfly
    sittin' in—
Willing to glow
    if the show's alive,
But if it dies
    it flies.

Montserrat, British West Indies   *October 1985*

A "men" from Amy,
An "A" from me,
staccato amens at the end,
mending tile of missing terra-cotta,
blending the suspension to the ground.
Tilting two ceramic bits of glaze,
two journeymen gaze at the sound
of reflected holy spirit,
angelic angles,
magical overtones,
dome of mosaic music.

Montserrat, British West Indies   *December 1985*

IV: FIRE

INTERVIEWER: How did *The Animals' Christmas* recording come about?

ART GARFUNKEL: *The Animals' Christmas* took up the middle of the Eighties for me; it finally came out in Christmas of '86 after four years of my performing it and then recording it. In the early Eighties, in September of 1981, Paul Simon and I did a concert in Central Park. We followed it by touring the world: a European tour, an Australian tour, a Japanese tour, and finally a baseball–stadium tour in the U.S.A. in the summer of '83. As that baseball–stadium tour was finishing with two Swiss shows and two shows in Israel, I knew that the future was mine. I was open to what would come next. That's how I began to write what became this book. And I also started *The Animals' Christmas*. In '83, my friend Jimmy Webb showed me a piece he was writing, a cantata for children's choir and small orchestra for his local church in Tuxedo, New York. And it being a noncommercial endeavor, I was particularly interested in it, because I had become cynical about the fact that the record business will professionalize one's musical attempts in a way that can hurt them. And I followed Jimmy's rehearsals in Tuxedo and loved *The Animals' Christmas*. I told him I wanted to get involved. By the next year, he had written an extension, doubled its length and wrote various sections for me as solo singer, narrator, and the angel Gabriel. He added a woman's part—the Virgin Mary. We all performed it with orchestra, children's choir, boy singer, girl singer, at St. John the Divine Cathedral that December in New York, and also at Festival Hall in London. We made a live recording of the show, which later seemed to me too loose. So we planned to record it in the studio, the following Christmas. I started in London in '85 and recorded the London Symphony Orchestra; we added the choir from Wimbledon that winter; come the spring I was in Montserrat doing my vocals with Geoff Emerick; I traveled to Nashville to get Amy Grant's vocals on the album, then came to New York for some percussion overdubs—Steve Gadd on drums, and others. I had it finished by Christmas of '86, which I gather is when it came out. It's a gothic cathedral of an album; it's very ambitious. It was the type of project that would have been done by papal commission long ago.

I: So it was a very satisfying experience?
AG: Some artistic endeavors are more committed than others. You try to run the full mile with everything; sometimes you really get to do it. That was one of those times. Another was doing *Bad Timing,* the movie I made with Nic Roeg. That was a ferocious "race for the gold."

I: You use the line "Tomorrow it's over. Tonight is all." Do you feel this every time you perform?
AG: Yes. When you're onstage, that time is an island. We don't normally spend our lives with the spirit called forth and flowing, coming up and out; it's a wonderful ecstasy to be there.

I: It sounds wonderful.
AG: It *is* wonderful; it's a very lucky thing.

66

Wintertime nighs. Perhaps I'll light a fire this year. Maybe I'll put away her things.

New York City   *November 1985*

67

Cooperation breeds contempt for all the required restraint. In the fruitless pursuit of the dovetail, we inevitably chip a fingernail on the lie in the logistics of fitting in. Who doesn't know the overawareness of two heads bumping to pick up a pin, the flutter of the abdomen, living in check, say cheeese?

There's a series of overtones, I believe, coloring converse in human affairs: when she looks in his eyes . . . does she see that he knows that she knows that he sees (for these are the overtones) or does she just look at his face—that fundamental wavelength—aharmonic—without the tone of personality—perhaps a discrepancy between her very sound and his?

And so there really *is* a place for war in our hearts, for the thrusted truth, the scary disruption, upheaval, eruption of identity, a personal call—that which makes us really not the same at all.

Les Arcs, France   *January 1986*

68

Life is fixed in soulfire;
Only the physical fades away.

Today and the end-of-winter wind
bring tears to my weakening eyes.
The squinting of winter buds.
Do we renew?

I think of my father westering,
of his ancient watery eyes,
tremulous, brimming with sentiment.

As if to receive the eyecup,
I tilt my head and walk amid the film.
Then return to my room.
The gardenia plant has passed its bloom.
All is green.
The wink of spring.

Awash in wonder I water it,
awaiting the white again.

New York City   March 1986

Before she died she went to Bali, tilting the global balance. She was gorgeous for others. A photographer took a picture of her in a pool in a glade in the nude. Perhaps she swam for him . . . then water must have rushed between her thighs. Then did she dip her porcelain head and rise in undulation, arched in exhibition—mysterious, cruel— late for the sky and the wild swans at Coole?

Les Arcs, France   *January 1986*

my dad
(an apologetic man)
a creature of old paltry habits
ardentest heart of all.
He couldn't accept that his eyes were bad
    because they had done their term.
He feared to sell the house he made so
    permanent.

—I want to be alive to do it, he told me,
My books, my life, coins in a drawer,
Fans tramping through the door.

I believe, with my brother, this summer
        The Mason went home to his house to die.
He dealt with the dentist,
        he kinda liked living alone, until
One day Mrs. Slammowitz came to collect—
        a real estate broker, nothing more
            (what was he apologizing for?)

I believe he took the stairs too fast
        when he went up for the check.

New York City   *September 1986*

103

71

Work and its regimen
presses the piper
compresses the oxygen
gives it potential thrust—
latent spending,
kinetic thrift;
Nick is the air that blows through the port
and underarms for lift.

                         Dusk in the harbor of old Marseille.
His apartment, up a hill, a block away. Off with our shoes—
suffused in sensuality, we sprawl on the carpet of the attic loft.
Isabelle, the girl he sleeps with, is there. But his relationship is
in each of his narrow shoulders' awareness of the other, and
mine is there with his, and with the weight of his slightly
parted indolent lips. (*beau d'abandon*) Will I get him a pack of
Camels? (just to buy him something is sublime) I'm out the
door down to the street into the Mediterraneanair leaping the
street stairs arms and feet—unable to take them one at a time.

Marseille, France   *September 1986*

104

72

my fingers wrapped around his thumb
his hand enclosing mine—we meet
held in the harbor between our hearts
pressed against the bottom sheet—
waves of approval caress the boat
across the bay with every beat

Merano, Italy   March 1986

73

Lourdes is heavy and so am I,
laden with lost opportunity.
Prêt is ready to sing the blues,
but I am lingering in Toulouse.
Heaven can wait with the SNCF,
I am out for the evening news.

O what joy
it is to walk
upon the earth
by the waterside
To be with the living
and with all things alive
To be able to fly and have life.

Toulouse, France   *September 1986*

106

74

Most of my love life's been given to
    acquiescence.
But the essence of loving—the seed inbred
    is the wanting to be with the one you love
And the feeding of the need that must be fed.

We lingered a lot in bed that week—a pair
    of expatriate artists with jam on the spread;
We smoked cigarettes in our underwear
    until all of the Austrian *Herald Tribune*
    had been read.

What did we know of the proper forms of love?
Then it was magic—you could pretend
    a friend was a lover who loved you when
    you'd thirst for what you must have, in the
    end.

St. Anton, Austria   *March 1986*

75

Prepare to leave me now.
Leave me in the stream of being, struggling for
faith; project-prone and lonely, a film in the can, an
album near-complete.

De "l'âme de l'oiseau"
to *Good to Go,* from Berne to Moscow, Tahiti to
Moline, the meaning in the noun

celebration

A person, place or thing I gave my heart to. Lisa
under the equator in moonlight, Kim in my arms, in
the center of the womb, literature in a hotel room,
the hermit crab, the end of a limb, foam thrown
back by the wave, autumnal, agnostic archer of two
cords, in love with arctic Aphrodite still.

Hollywood   November 1985

76

Two ducks on a foot-square pond, yellow on blue, have been sitting on my kitchen table for something like eight or nine years. One holds sugar, the other is empty, time gliding by the three of us.

I visit my friend in the country. He's made some additions in the last few years—a wing on the house, species of trees, a pond. Under the dazzling morning sun, the two of us sit by the pond and sip coffee. Lost love is the refrain unspoken, yet we remain the wishful chorus. Two ducks, tied together, drift in time before us.

Amagansett, N.Y.   September 1986

77

On a wall in my parents' house is a photograph of the Wailing Wall. A tall man, wearing a *tallis* with his back to us in the noon sun, stands before the massive wall of Jerusalem. As if a wail would escape from him to defy the scale of the stone—only to find atonement therein.

I met a Cleopatra in a hotel pool in Tel Aviv. Several years have passed since then. Tonight I dine with my heart on my sleeve in the Chestnut Room of the Tavern on the Green. I sit in between my girlfriend and boyfriend and order a beer . . . she's shy with him . . . I go to Jerusalem, back to the wall, I feel through veneer and the years of assimilation—that the girl is here!

New York City   January 1987

110

78

I drifted north on the first day off
to look at the Londoners,
air up the ailerons,
track the topography,
feel England rise from the Thames.
Marylebone Station . . . Wellington Road . . .
Noon at the ridge of North End Way.

A particular type of Romantic
will praise the Hampstead Heath—
those who love the upland view,
those few of you with eyes that roam
over the St. Paul dome to Byzantium

I carry on down the northern slope.
View is lost, all guiding signs are gone,
but one:
High above the heath,
beneath a cloudy day,
two lines askew converge for you
in skywriting.
What does it mean?
The Byzantine beyond the Adriatic art?

O Poor Heart
You are lost. Earth eludes.
You are left with skyward moorings.

London   March 1988

79

In London twenty years ago
in St. James's Park at the break of dawn,
Paul and I and Beverly
were easing down from an all-night high.

Microscopic organisms
alter their behavior
when a scientist is watching.
Everything waits to be noticed:
a tree falling with no one there,
the full potential of a love affair,
twenty-eight geese in sudden flight . . .

London   September 1987

Jess,
the synthesizer player in the band,
took me into commonwealth curriculum—
U.K. Psych. course, one-o-one:
self-awareness,
objective-, subjective-style.

Say you're in the middle of a song on stage
and thousands of people are watching you—
the wrong thing to do
is to fix on the question:
"What's my next line?"
That's objective.
It's a land mine.

But to push the awareness away and just be
(remember me to one who lives there)
and dare to bare your living doubt,
to let out the indwelling heart for a while—
that's the subjective style.

To video or not is now the question:
whether it's better to know what we look like
before the finale and gain that awareness
                                    thereby,

or carry on from town to town
in trusted illusion, subjectively speaking
blindness is bliss . . .
It comes to this:

It's not one of a pair
and the part one picks.
The self, aware, knows
the art of the mix.

London   April 1988

81

Why couldn't I be a goldsmith? I could build an entire battle scene in little strips of filigree with separate strands of gold in the horses' manes and set it all on a pinky ring for Anjelica's adornment . . . and not have to sing these nuances, inviting angels on to the head of a pin.

Montauk, N.Y.   *September 1986*

82

Nobody sees the welder.
No one can face the brilliant light
    he works with.
In the city of Zurich by the river's quay,
a welder lifts his shield and looks at me.
The river shimmers to the Zurichsee.
Night has fallen.
Autumn has come.
    "The air is a dove which,
    as it rests on its nest,
    keeps its young warm."

What did you sing there? What did you note?
What did you see with your
    thrush in the throat?

I saw a boy painted ivory who stood like
    a statue;
saw another boy fix a syringe by the river.
I saw chasms so holy the heart was arrested;
I saw curves in the earth—
    the caress of my hand
    o'er the hairs of her thigh
    in the lay of the land.
Saw a girl at the window,
saw lumps in the meadows,
rode up the Alps with her,
    bonded through conifer,
    married to liberty,
    over the Albula Pass.
Three years have passed . . .

Last night I ate bone marrow at the
    Central Hotel . . . tenderness . . .
    remembrance of things . . .
    Laurie of the Orient
    a motherless birth . . .
Because of the infant in her arms,
a mother waves her love at a passing train.
I leave this train at Bergün
    to kiss the miraculous earth.

Bergün, Switzerland   September 1986

83

There she'd be beside me in our big brass bed looking southwest down into Central Park. Shiny from her bath, she'd wear pale orange parachute material. I'd be reading, she'd be singing her scales, wrinkling her infant pink nose, and slaying me by singing through it:

"nee, nee, nee, nee . . .

New York City   June 1985

84

Soon I will rise onto the mesa,
Play on the tableland under the lights.
Three nights at the Royal Albert Hall.

All my aspiration . . . All aspire . . .
The morning sky on the high plateau, afire.

Enter the pop warrior.
Held in thrall to seven tiers,
"Hello darkness" for twenty-four years.

Be beautiful. Be a man.
Do what no one can.
Stand for genetic union.
Be mild in a battle blaze.

Go out on the field of praise to the apron.
Tell every stall: tomorrow it's over.
Tonight is all.

London   April 1988

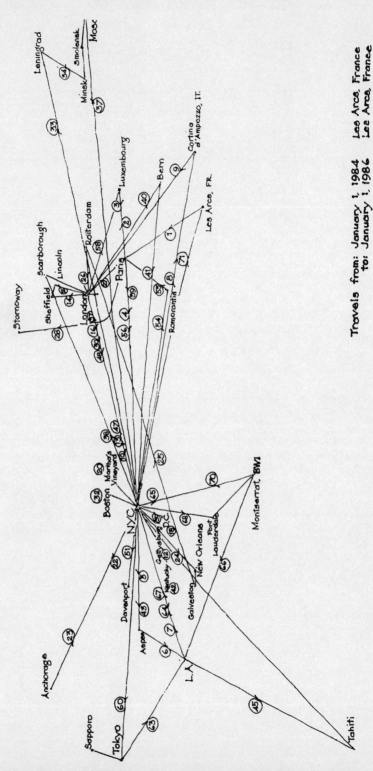

Travels from: January 1, 1984   Les Arcs, France
to: January 1, 1986   Les Arcs, France